From the heart of the Founder & Developer of C.A.P.E. [Courageously Affirming & Protecting through Education] Curriculum…

Thank you for investing in the safety and well-being of the students you have been privileged to influence. Undoubtedly, education is the tool that necessitates every human being to do *more*! C.A.P.E. Curriculum is designed to do more than educate, it will teach students of all ages how to affirm and protect themselves by utilizing the very thing that is silenced most often– their voice! This curriculum has been developed for the specialized need of social awareness and social activism to help prevent bullying, sexual abuse and illegal drug use in children, early on. C.A.P.E. Curriculum is designed based upon Next Generation Sunshine State Standards for health and social education. These can be found at CPALMS.org. In addition, the standards can be easily adapted to Common Core Standards. Common Core has been implemented in more than 40 states in the U.S. and the District of Columbia. The standards are research and evidence based, which are clear, understandable and consistent. They are also aligned with other top performing countries in order to prepare students for success on a global scale.

Due to the unfortunate and alarmingly increase in preventable violations against children and adolescents, C.A.P.E. Curriculum is not only a wise investment but a vital investment. As educators, we are obligated to help ensure that our students are prepared for life in all capacities. Consequently, this curriculum allows educators to approach sensitive issues from an empowered position. Each lesson offers simplistic yet profound directions to help students protect themselves from situations and people that can be detrimental to their growth [educationally, emotionally, mentally and socially].

I know C.A.P.E. Curriculum will incite "COURAGEous Conversations™" and provide the educational empowerment that is desperately needed to aid in the prevention of harmful acts and situations involving our youth. I am humbled and elated that you have chosen C.A.P.E. Curriculum as an educational tool. I am confident that it will impact your students long after the school day has ended and years following high school graduation. Additionally, this curriculum will empower students to become their own advocate by activating their superpower–courage–to help ensure there are *no surprises, just courage*!™

Courageously yours,

Kandra C. Albury

Advocate, Author, Conqueror and Sexual Abuse Prevention Educator

Copyright © 2019 by Kandra Albury, MA, Ph.D.

All rights reserved. No part of this publication may be reproduced, distributed, or transmitted in any form or by any means, including photocopying, recording, or other electronic or mechanical methods, without the prior written permission of the publisher, except in the case of brief quotations embodied in critical reviews and certain other noncommercial uses permitted by copyright law. However, copies may be made of supplemental learning materials for classroom/continual educational use. Questions or requests should be directed to: kidsncapes.inc@gmail.com.

The Feisty Four Children's Book Series is available online at Amazon, Barnes & Noble, Books-A-Million and Walmart.

www.kidsncapesinc.org

ISBN1: 978-1-7335709-6-1

C.A.P.E. Curriculum
Table of Contents

Health Education Standards Adapted to C.A.P.E. Curriculum & COURAGEous
Conversations ™ 1

C.A.P.E .Curriculum – Sexual Abuse Awareness & Prevention Unit Outline/Specifications 3

    Sexual Abuse Awareness & Prevention – Focused Lesson #1 4
    Sexual Abuse Awareness & Prevention – Focused Lesson #2 5
    Sexual Abuse Awareness & Prevention – Focused Lesson #3 6
    Sexual Abuse Awareness & Prevention – Focused Lesson #4 7

C.A.P.E. Curriculum – Bullying Awareness & Prevention Unit Outline/Specifications 9

    Bullying Awareness & Prevention – Focused Lesson #5 10
    Bullying Awareness & Prevention – Focused Lesson #6 11
    Bullying Awareness & Prevention – Focused Lesson #7 12
    Bullying Awareness & Prevention – Focused Lesson #8 13

C.A.P.E. Curriculum – Drug Use Awareness & Prevention Unit Outline/Specifications 15

    Illegal Drug Use Awareness & Prevention – Focused Lesson #9 16
    Illegal Drug Use Awareness & Prevention – Focused Lesson #10 17
    Illegal Drug Use Awareness & Prevention – Focused Lesson #11 18
    Illegal Drug Use Awareness & Prevention – Focused Lesson #12 19

C.A.P.E. Curriculum – Courageous Power of Using Your Voice Unit Outline/Specifications 21

    The Courageous Power of Using Your Voice – Focused Lesson #13 22
    The Courageous Power of Using Your Voice – Focused Lesson #14 23
    The Courageous Power of Using Your Voice – Focused Lesson #15 24
    The Courageous Power of Using Your Voice – Focused Lesson #16 25

COURAGEous Conversation™ for Adolescents – For Secondary Education 26

    COURAGEous Conversation™: How to Avoid or Overcome Sexual Abuse 27
    COURAGEous Conversation™: How to Avoid or Overcome Bullies or
        Bullying Situations 32
    COURAGEous Conversation™ : How to Avoid Drug Use & Being Influenced by Others
        with the Pressure of Trying Drugs 35

APPENDICES

A	DYDTMT Zones Information Sheet	39
B.	DYDTMT Zones - Identification Activity Sheet (Girls)	40
C.	DYDTMT Zones - Identification Activity Sheet (Boys)	41
D.	Different Types of Bullying – Identification Activity Sheet	42
E.	How Drugs Affect Your Body – Identification Activity Sheet	43
F.	Snitching/Tattling Versus Telling – Identification Activity Sheet	44
G.	COURAGEous™ Declarations (Body Safety)	45
H.	COURAGEous Tween Talk ™ Q&A	46

I.	COURAGEous™ Declarations (Anti-Bullying)	47
J.	COURAGEous™ Declarations (Anti-Drug Abuse)	48
K.	Parental Permission Slip	49
L.	The Promise to Tell & Listen Agreement ("Don't You Dare Touch Me There!")	50
M.	The Promise to Tell & Listen Agreement ("Leave Us Alone You Mean 'Ole Bully!")	51
N.	The Pledge to be Drug Free ("NO… And I Mean No! Let's Say No to Drugs!")	52
O.	The Promise to Tell & Listen Agreement (Be COURAGEous™ – Speak Up and Speak Out!)	53
P.	My Heroic Rights to be Brave!	54
Q.	Songs & Chants to enCOURAGE	55
R.	Statistical Data Regarding Children About Sexual Abuse, Bullying, & Drug Usage	56
S.	Resources for Help	57

Works Cited 58

Health Education Standards Adapted to C.A.P.E. Curriculum & COURAGEous Conversations ™

Health Education Standards – Elementary & Secondary Education	
HE.K.C.1.1 –	Recognize healthy behaviors.
HE.1.C.1.1 –	Identify healthy behaviors.
HE.1.C.1.5 –	Identify the correct names of human body parts.
HE.123.C.2.2 –	Recognize, explore, and describe the ways that a friend would act in a variety of situations.
HE.2.C.1.1 –	Identify that healthy behaviors affect personal health.
HE.3.C.1.1 –	Describe & identify healthy behaviors that affect personal health.
HE.4.C.1.3 –	Describe & identify practices for a safe, healthy environment that promote personal health.
HE.45.C.1.4 –	Describe & identify ways to prevent childhood injuries and health problems.
HE.6.C.1.2 –	Describe how the physical, mental/emotional, social, and intellectual dimensions of health are interrelated.
HE.7.C.1.1 –	Compare and contrast the effects of healthy and unhealthy behaviors on personal health, including sexual and emotional health.
HE.7.C.1.4 –	Describe ways to reduce or prevent injuries and adolescent health problems.
HE.678.C.1.4 –	Identify, describe, and investigate ways to reduce or prevent harm/injuries and adolescent health problems- emotionally, socially, and physically.
HE.8.C.1.2 –	Analyze the interrelationship between healthy/unhealthy behaviors and the dimensions of health: physical, mental/emotional, social.
HE.678.C.1.6 –	Examine, explain, and analyze how appropriate health practices/care can promote personal health.
HE.678.C.1.8 –	Examine, explain, and analyze the likelihood of injury or illness if engaging in unhealthy/risky behaviors.
HE.912.C.1.1 –	Predict how healthy behaviors can affect health status.
HE.912.C.1.4 –	Propose strategies to reduce or prevent injuries and health problems.
HE.912.C.1.8 –	Assess the degree of susceptibility to injury, illness or death if engaging in unhealthy/risky behaviors.

BODY SAFETY

Sexual Abuse Prevention & Awareness

Lessons:

* Understanding & Preventing Inappropriate Touching.

* The Importance of Speaking UP for Yourself, TELL!

* If Something Inappropriate Happens, It Is NOT Your Fault.

* Be Courageous! Courage is YOUR Super-Power!

C.A.P.E. Curriculum – Sexual Abuse Awareness & Prevention Unit
Outline & Specifications

Unit: Sexual Abuse Awareness & Prevention

Standards:

HE.K.C.1.1 – Recognize healthy behaviors.

HE.123.C.2.2 – Recognize, explore, and describe the ways that a friend would act in a variety of situations.

HE.3.C.1.1 – Describe & identify healthy behaviors that affect personal health.

HE.4.C.1.3 – Describe ways a safe, healthy environment can promote personal health.

HE.45.C.1.4 – Describe & identify ways to prevent childhood injuries and health problems.

Lessons:

1. Understanding & Preventing Inappropriate Touching.
2. The Importance of Speaking Up for Yourself, Tell!
3. *If* Something Inappropriate Happens, It Is Not Your Fault.
4. Be Courageous! Courage is Your Super-Power!

Lesson Plan:

Direct Teaching/Introduction to the Lesson: Start each lesson as a discussion by prompting student engagement and thinking with the guiding questions. Allow the students to answer briefly. Introduce the specified anchor text, pass around the "Capes of Courage," and identify the DYDTMT [Don't You Dare Touch Me There} Zones. Then read the specified anchor text as a "read-a-loud" (be as animated as possible). Stop and check for student understanding, pause if any students appear to be confused and ensure their comprehension.

Collaborative Learning and/or Independent Learning:

Activity 1: Independent Learning: Identification Worksheet – "DYDTMT" Body Zones

Activity 2: Collaborative Practice: "Always Tell" – retell scenarios from "Don't You Dare Touch Me There!" Then have students hypothetically act out or tell what they would do in the situation.

Activity 3: Collaborative Practice: "Showing Empathy & Concern" retell scenarios from "Don't You Dare Touch Me There." Then have students hypothetically act out or tell what they would do in the situation.

Activity 4: Cooperative Learning: Students will complete "The Promise to Tell and Listen Agreement."

Cooperative Closure for the Lessons:

Have the students journal or openly discuss their feelings regarding the lessons. If the students desire to share, encourage them to do so. Be mindful of student reactions to the lessons, and remember your classroom should be a safety zone for all students.

C.A.P.E. Curriculum – Lesson(s) 1-4:
Sexual Abuse Awareness & Prevention

Title:	Sexual Abuse Awareness & Prevention – LESSON 1
Grade level:	Pre-K – 5
Subject(s):	Health Education
Specific topic:	Understanding & Preventing Inappropriate Touching.
Lesson Timeframe:	25-50 minutes (dependent upon grade level)

Summary
This lesson will aid students in understanding how to stop unwanted touching. Complete activity 1.

Guiding Question(s)
What is "good" touching? What is bad touching? What should you do, if someone tries to touch you in a "don't-touch zone?"

Standards Assessed in the Learning Expedition		
Discipline	Standards	Long-Term Learning Targets
Health Education	HE.2.C.1.2 – Recognize physical, mental/emotional & social dimensions of health.	Understand appropriate personal space & recognize abusive behaviors.

C.A.P.E. Curriculum Anchor Text(s): *Anchor texts are key texts read to support content and health education skills. A teacher's set of the anchor texts are highly recommended.*

Title	Author/Illustrator	Text Type
Don't You Dare Touch Me There!	Kandra Albury/Jamie Cosley	Instructional Fiction

C.A.P.E. Curriculum – Lesson(s) 1-4:
Sexual Abuse Awareness & Prevention

Title:	Sexual Abuse Awareness & Prevention – LESSON 2
Grade level:	Pre-K – 5
Subject(s):	Health Education
Specific topic:	The Importance of Speaking Up for Yourself, Tell!
Lesson Timeframe:	25-50 minutes (dependent upon grade level)

Summary
This lesson will help students understand why telling/speaking-up for themselves is the most POWERFUL skill against harmful situations and people.

Guiding Question(s)
Are secrets "bad?" When shouldn't an action or something someone says, not be a secret? What should you do, if someone says, "Don't tell, it's our secret…" or "No one will believe you" but you feel uncomfortable?

Standards Assessed in the Learning Expedition		
Discipline	Standards	Long-Term Learning Targets
Health Education	HE.1.C.1.4 – Identify ways to prevent harm/injuries in the home, school, and community settings.	Understand and practice the skill of openly expressing a problem.

C.A.P.E. Curriculum Anchor Text(s): *Anchor texts are key texts read to support content and health education skills. A teacher's set of the anchor texts are highly recommended.*		
Title	Author/Illustrator	Text Type
Don't You Dare Touch Me There!	Kandra Albury/Jamie Cosley	Instructional Fiction

C.A.P.E. Curriculum – Lesson(s) 1-4:
Sexual Abuse Awareness & Prevention

Title:	**Sexual Abuse Awareness & Prevention – LESSON 3**
Grade level:	Pre-K – 5
Subject(s):	Health Education
Specific topic:	*If* Something Inappropriate Happens, It's Not Your Fault.
Lesson Timeframe:	25-50 minutes (dependent upon grade level)

Summary
This lesson will help students understand that as children they are not to be blamed or at fault because of someone else's actions.

Guiding Question(s)
Do people *always* do what is right? Is it your fault if someone does something that hurts you or makes you feel uncomfortable?

Standards Assessed in the Learning Expedition		
Discipline	**Standards**	**Long-Term Learning Targets**
Health Education	HE.4.C.1.2 – Identify examples of mental/emotional, physical, and social health.	Understand and practice the skill of openly expressing a problem.

C.A.P.E. Curriculum Anchor Text(s): *Anchor texts are key texts read to support content and health education skills. A teacher's set of the anchor texts are highly recommended.*		
Title	**Author/Illustrator**	**Text Type**
Don't You Dare Touch Me There!	Kandra Albury/Jamie Cosley	Instructional Fiction

C.A.P.E. Curriculum – Lesson(s) 1-4:
Sexual Abuse Awareness & Prevention

Title:	Sexual Abuse Awareness & Prevention – LESSON 4
Grade level:	Pre-K – 5
Subject(s):	Health Education
Specific topic:	Be COURAGEous! Courage is Your Super-power!
Lesson Timeframe:	25-50 minutes (dependent upon grade level)

Summary
This lesson will help students understand that it takes COURAGE to say and do something to STOP someone from harming them.

Guiding Question(s)
What does it mean to be courageous/brave? Does everyone have the ability to be COURAGEGOUS? Is it okay to be afraid and courageous at the same time?

Standards Assessed in the Learning Expedition			
Discipline	**Standards**	**Long-Term Learning Targets**
Health Education	HE.2.C.1.1 – Identify/practice healthy behaviors because they affect personal health.	Understand and practice the skill of being courageous constantly.

C.A.P.E. Curriculum Anchor Text(s): *Anchor texts are key texts read to support content and health education skills. A teacher's set of the anchor texts are highly recommended.*

Title	Author/Illustrator	Text Type
Don't You Dare Touch Me There!	Kandra Albury/Jamie Cosley	Instructional Fiction

~~BULLYING~~

Bullying Prevention + Awareness

Lessons:

* What Is Bullying + What Should You Do if it Happens to You.

* Understanding the Types of Bullying - Physical Intimidation and Verbal Intimidation!

* Bullying Is Never Acceptable.

* Be Courageous! Courage is Your Super-Power!

C.A.P.E. Curriculum – Bullying Awareness & Prevention Unit Outline & Specifications

Unit: Bullying Awareness & Prevention

Standards:

HE.K.C.1.1 – Recognize healthy behaviors.

HE.123.C.2.2 – Recognize, explore, and describe the ways that a friend would act in a variety of situations.

HE.3.C.1.1 – Describe & identify healthy behaviors that affect personal health.

HE.4.C.1.3 – Describe ways a safe, healthy environment can promote personal health.

HE.45.C.1.4 – Describe & identify ways to prevent childhood injuries and health problems.

Lessons:

1. What Is Bullying & What Should You Do *if* it Happens to You.
2. Understanding the Types of Bullying – Physical Intimidation and Verbal Intimidation!
3. Bullying Is Never Acceptable.
4. Be Courageous! Courage is Your Super-Power!

Lesson Plan:

Direct Teaching/Introduction to the Lesson: Start each lesson as a discussion by prompting student engagement and thinking with the guiding questions. Allow the students to answer briefly. Introduce the specified anchor text and pass around the "Capes of Courage." Read the text as a "read-a-loud" (be as animated as possible). Stop and check for student understanding, pause if any students seem confused and ensure their comprehension.

Collaborative Learning and/or Independent Learning:

Activity 1: Independent Learning: Identification Worksheet - "Different Types of Bullying"

Activity 2: Collaborative Practice: "Always Tell" – retell scenarios from "Leave Us Alone You Mean 'Ole Bully" Then have students hypothetically act out or tell what they would do in the situation.

Activity 3: Collaborative Practice: "Showing Empathy & Concern" retell scenarios from "Leave Us Alone You Mean Ole' Bully!" Then have students hypothetically act out or tell what they would do in the situation.

Activity 4: Cooperative Learning: Students will complete "The Promise NOT to Bully and Promise to Tell Agreement."

Cooperative Closure for the Lessons:

Have the students journal or openly discuss their feelings regarding the lessons. If the students desire to share, encourage them to do so. Be mindful of student reactions to the lessons, and remember your classroom should be a safety zone for all students.

C.A.P.E. Curriculum – Lesson(s) 5-8:
Bullying Awareness & Prevention

Title:	Bullying Awareness & Prevention – LESSON 5
Grade level:	Pre-K – 5
Subject(s):	Health Education
Specific topic:	What Is Bullying, and What Should You Do, *if* it Happens to You.
Lesson Timeframe:	25-50 minutes (dependent upon grade level)

Summary
This lesson will help students understand what bullying *is* and how to protect themselves from bullies.

Guiding Question(s)
What is a Bully? Are there different kinds of bullying? What should you do *if* you feel or believe someone is bullying you?

Standards Assessed in the Learning Expedition		
Discipline	Standards	Long-Term Learning Targets
Health Education	HE.4.C.1.2 – Identify examples of mental/emotional, physical, and social health.	Understand and practice the skill of openly expressing a problem.

C.A.P.E. Curriculum Anchor Text(s): *Anchor texts are key texts read to support content and health education skills. A teacher's set of the anchor texts are highly recommended.*		
Title	Author/Illustrator	Text Type
Leave Us Alone You Mean 'Ole Bully!	Kandra Albury/Jamie Cosley	Instructional Fiction

C.A.P.E. Curriculum – Lesson(s) 5-8: Bullying Awareness & Prevention

Title:	Bullying Awareness & Prevention – LESSON 6
Grade level:	Pre-K – 5
Subject(s):	Health Education
Specific topic:	Understanding the Types of Bullying – Physical Intimidation and Verbal Intimidation!
Lesson Timeframe:	25-50 minutes (dependent upon grade level)

Summary
This lesson will help students understand and identify the various forms of bullying and how to protect themselves from bullies.

Guiding Question(s)
What does it mean to intimidate someone? What is more hurtful, words or hitting? Do you know anyone who was bullied or have you ever bullied anyone?

Standards Assessed in the Learning Expedition		
Discipline	Standards	Long-Term Learning Targets
Health Education	HE.4.C.1.2 – Identify examples of mental/emotional, physical, and social health.	Understand and practice the skill of openly expressing a problem.

C.A.P.E. Curriculum Anchor Text(s): *Anchor texts are key texts read to support content and health education skills. A teacher's set of the anchor texts are highly recommended.*

Title	Author/Illustrator	Text Type
Leave Us Alone You Mean 'Ole Bully!	Kandra Albury/Jamie Cosley	Instructional Fiction

C.A.P.E. Curriculum – Lesson(s) 5-8: Bullying Awareness & Prevention

Title:	Bullying Awareness & Prevention – LESSON 7
Grade level:	Pre-K – 5
Subject(s):	Health Education
Specific topic:	Bullying is Never Acceptable!
Lesson Timeframe:	25-50 minutes (dependent upon grade level)

Summary
This lesson will help students understand the effects of bullying and why it is an unacceptable practice/behavior.

Guiding Question(s)
Is it ever *okay* to bully someone? Is bullying a crime? What can you do to help someone who is being bullied?

Standards Assessed in the Learning Expedition		
Discipline	Standards	Long-Term Learning Targets
Health Education	HE.45.C.1.4 – Describe & identify ways to prevent childhood injuries and health problems.	Understand and practice the skill of openly expressing a problem.

C.A.P.E. Curriculum Anchor Text(s): *Anchor texts are key texts read to support content and health education skills. A teacher's set of the anchor texts are highly recommended.*

Title	Author/Illustrator	Text Type
Leave Us Alone You Mean 'Ole Bully!	Kandra Albury/Jamie Cosley	Instructional Fiction

C.A.P.E. Curriculum – Lesson(s) 5-8:
Bullying Awareness & Prevention

Title:	Bullying Awareness & Prevention – LESSON 8
Grade level:	Pre-K – 5
Subject(s):	Health Education
Specific topic:	Be COURAGEous, It's Your Super-Power!
Lesson Timeframe:	25-50 minutes (dependent upon grade level)

Summary
This lesson will help students understand the importance of speaking up about being bullied or witnessing an occurrence of bullying.

Guiding Question(s)
Do you like helping others? What are ways that we can help someone who is being mistreated? Even when we're afraid, can we still be courageous?

Standards Assessed in the Learning Expedition		
Discipline	Standards	Long-Term Learning Targets
Health Education	HE.4.C.1.3 – Describe & identify practices for a safe, healthy environment that promotes personal health.	Understand and practice the skill of openly expressing a problem.

C.A.P.E. Curriculum Anchor Text(s): *Anchor texts are key texts read to support content and health education skills. A teacher's set of the anchor texts are highly recommended.*

Title	Author/Illustrator	Text Type
Leave Us Alone You Mean 'Ole Bully!	Kandra Albury/Jamie Cosley	Instructional Fiction

~~DRUGS~~

Drug Abuse Prevention + Awareness

Lessons:

* What Are Drugs + What Should You Do If You Find Them or If Someone Offers Drugs to You?

* Understanding Why Drugs Are Harmful To You, Others, and Our Communities!

* Drug Abuse Is Always Dangerous.

* Be Courageous! Courage is Your Super-Power!

C.A.P.E. Curriculum –Drug Use Awareness & Prevention Unit
Outline and Specifications

Unit: Drug Use Awareness & Prevention

Standards:

HE.K.C.1.1 – Recognize healthy behaviors.

HE.2.C.1.1 – Identify that healthy behaviors affect personal health.

HE.3.C.1.1 – Describe & identify healthy behaviors that affect personal health.

HE.4.C.1.3 – Describe ways a safe, healthy environment can promote personal health.

HE.45.C.1.4 – Describe & identify ways to prevent childhood injuries and health problems.

Lessons:

1. What Are Drugs & What Should You Do *If* You Find Them or *If* Someone Offers Drugs to You?
2. Understanding Why Drugs Are Harmful – To You, Others, and Our Communities!
3. Drug Abuse Is Always Dangerous.
4. Be Courageous! Courage is Your Super-Power!

Lesson Plan:

Direct Teaching/Introduction to the Lesson: Start each lesson as a discussion by prompting student engagement and thinking with the guiding questions. Allow the students to answer briefly. Introduce the specified anchor text and pass around the "Capes of Courage." Read the text as a "read-a-loud" (be as animated as possible). Stop and check for student understanding, pause if any students seem confused and ensure their comprehension.

Collaborative Learning and/or Independent Learning:

Activity 1: Independent Learning: Identification Worksheet – "How Drugs Affect Your Body"

Activity 2: Collaborative Practice: "Always Say NO" – retell scenarios from "NO! … And I Mean NO, Let's Say No to Drugs!" Then have students hypothetically act out or tell what they would do in the situation.

Activity 3: Independent Practice/Collaborative Discussion: "Courageous Declarations" have students complete the corresponding activity sheet. Students will write and recite various ways to say "NO" to drugs!

Activity 4: Cooperative Learning: Students will complete "The Pledge to Be Drug-Free Agreement."

Cooperative Closure for the Lessons:

Have the students journal or openly discuss their feelings regarding the lessons. If the students desire to share, encourage them to do so. Be mindful of student reactions to the lessons, and remember your classroom should be a safety zone for all students.

C.A.P.E. Curriculum – Lesson(s) 9-12: Drug Use Awareness & Prevention

Title:	**Drug Use Awareness & Prevention – LESSON 9**
Grade level:	Pre-K – 5
Subject(s):	Health Education
Specific topic:	What Are Drugs & What Should You Do *If* You Find Them or Someone Offers Drugs to You?
Lesson Timeframe:	25-50 minutes (dependent upon grade level)

Summary
This lesson will help students recognize harmful substances (drugs) and teach them how to say NO if drugs are offered to them.

Guiding Question(s)
What are drugs? What is the difference between illegal and legal drugs? How do we tell a "friend" no when they try to convince us to do something that we know is wrong?

Standards Assessed in the Learning Expedition		
Discipline	Standards	Long-Term Learning Targets
Health Education	**HE.45.C.1.4** – Describe & identify ways to prevent childhood injuries and health problems.	Understand and practice the skill of being openly expressive about a problem or disagreeing with harmful or wrong behaviors/practices.

C.A.P.E. Curriculum Anchor Text(s): *Anchor texts are key texts read to support content and health education skills. A teacher's set of the anchor texts are highly recommended.*

Title	Author/Illustrator	Text Type
"NO! … And I Mean NO, Let's Say No to Drugs!"	Kandra Albury/Jamie Cosley	Instructional Fiction

C.A.P.E. Curriculum – Lesson(s) 9-12: Drug Use Awareness & Prevention

Title:	Drug Use Awareness & Prevention – LESSON 10
Grade level:	Pre-K – 5
Subject(s):	Health Education
Specific topic:	Understanding Why Drugs Are Harmful – To You, Others, and Our Communities!
Lesson Timeframe:	25-50 minutes (dependent upon grade level)

Summary
This lesson will help students understand the harmful effects of drugs.

Guiding Question(s)
Why are drugs harmful? Do drugs only effect the person who uses them or everyone around them? Even if a substance/drug is legal to use, can it still be harmful? How do we protect ourselves and others from drugs?

Standards Assessed in the Learning Expedition		
Discipline	Standards	Long-Term Learning Targets
Health Education	HE.45.C.1.4 – Describe & identify ways to prevent childhood injuries and health problems.	Understand and practice the skill of being openly expressive about a problem or disagreeing with harmful or wrong behaviors/practices.

C.A.P.E. Curriculum Anchor Text(s): *Anchor texts are key texts read to support content and health education skills. A teacher's set of the anchor texts are highly recommended.*		
Title	Author/Illustrator	Text Type
"NO! ... And I Mean NO, Let's Say No to Drugs!"	Kandra Albury/Jamie Cosley	Instructional Fiction

C.A.P.E. Curriculum – Lesson(s) 9-12:
Drug Use Awareness & Prevention

Title:	**Drug Use Awareness & Prevention – LESSON 11**
Grade level:	Pre-K – 5
Subject(s):	Health Education
Specific topic:	Drug Abuse Is Always Dangerous.
Lesson Timeframe:	25-50 minutes (dependent upon grade level)

Summary
This lesson will help students understand why drug abuse is always dangerous.

Guiding Question(s)
How can a <u>legal</u> substance (drug) be dangerous? What does it mean to abuse drugs? What should you do if you see someone using drugs? What happens to our bodies if we use drugs?

Standards Assessed in the Learning Expedition		
Discipline	Standards	Long-Term Learning Targets
Health Education	HE.45.C.1.4 – Describe & identify ways to prevent childhood injuries and health problems.	Understand and practice the skill of being openly expressive about a problem or disagreeing with harmful or wrong behaviors/practices.

C.A.P.E. Curriculum Anchor Text(s): *Anchor texts are key texts read to support content and health education skills. A teacher's set of the anchor texts are highly recommended.*		
Title	Author/Illustrator	Text Type
"NO! … And I Mean NO, Let's Say No to Drugs!"	Kandra Albury/Jamie Cosley	Instructional Fiction

C.A.P.E. Curriculum – Lesson(s) 9-12: Drug Use Awareness & Prevention

Title:	**Drug Use Awareness & Prevention – LESSON 12**
Grade level:	Pre-K – 5
Subject(s):	Health Education
Specific topic:	Be Courageous, It's Your Super-Power!
Lesson Timeframe:	25-50 minutes (dependent upon grade level)

Summary
This lesson will help students understand the importance of taking a stand against things that are wrong or make them feel uncomfortable, afraid, or uncertain.

Guiding Question(s)
What do you do if someone says, "Try it, one time, it won't hurt?" If we feel afraid, nervous, or unsure, how can we still activate our superpower courage? What is the most powerful possession you have to STOP behaviors that are wrong?

Standards Assessed in the Learning Expedition		
Discipline	Standards	Long-Term Learning Targets
Health Education	**HE.45.C.1.4** – Describe & identify ways to prevent childhood injuries and health problems.	Understand and practice the skill of being openly expressive about a problem or disagreeing with harmful or wrong behaviors/practices.

C.A.P.E. Curriculum Anchor Text(s): *Anchor texts are key texts read to support content and health education skills. A teacher's set of the anchor texts are highly recommended.*

Title	Author/Illustrator	Text Type
NO! … And I Mean NO, Let's Say No to Drugs!"	Kandra Albury/Jamie Cosley	Instructional Fiction

SPEAK UP!
The Courageous Power of Using Your Voice

Lessons:

* It's Not Your Fault.

* What to Do When a Family Member or Friend Violates Your Trust.

* It's Not Tattling When You're Trying to Protect Yourself or Someone Else.

* Be Courageous! Courage is Your Super-Power!

C.A.P.E. Curriculum – The Courageous Power of Using Your Voice
Unit Outline & Specifications

Unit: The Courageous Power of Using Your Voice

Standards:

HE.K.C.1.1 – Recognize healthy behaviors.

HE.2.C.1.1 – Identify that healthy behaviors affect personal health.

HE.3.C.1.1 – Describe & identify healthy behaviors that affect personal health.

HE.4.C.1.3 – Describe ways a safe, healthy environment can promote personal health.

HE.45.C.1.4 – Describe & identify ways to prevent childhood injuries and health problems.

Lessons:

1. It's Not Your Fault.
2. What to Do When a Family Member or Friend Violates Your Trust.
3. It's Not Tattling *When* You're Trying to Protect Yourself or Someone Else.
4. Be Courageous! Courage is Your Super-Power!

Lesson Plan:

Direct Teaching/Introduction to the Lesson: Start each lesson as a discussion by prompting student engagement and thinking with the guiding questions. Allow the students to answer briefly. Introduce the specified anchor text and pass around the "Capes of Courage." Read the text as a "read-a-loud" (be as animated as possible). Stop and check for student understanding, pause if any students seem confused and ensure their comprehension.

Collaborative Learning and/or Independent Learning:

Activity 1: Independent Learning: Identification Worksheet – "Tattling Versus Tattling/Snitching"

Activity 2: Collaborative Practice: "Always Tell/Speak Up" – retell scenarios from "You Did It Not Me! Brave Brittany Speaks Up!" Then have students hypothetically act out or tell what they would do in the situation.

Activity 3: Independent Practice/Collaborative Discussion: "Courageous Declarations" have students complete the corresponding activity sheet. Students will write and recite various ways to say "I've been violated!"

Activity 4: Cooperative Learning: Students will complete "The Promise to Tell & Listen Agreement."

Cooperative Closure for the Lessons:

Have the students journal or openly discuss their feelings regarding the lessons. If the students desire to share, encourage them to do so. Be mindful of student reactions to the lessons, and remember your classroom should be a safety zone for all students.

C.A.P.E. Curriculum – Lesson(s) 13-16:
The Courageous Power of Using Your Voice

Title:	Drug Use Awareness & Prevention – LESSON 13
Grade level:	Pre-K – 5
Subject(s):	Health Education
Specific topic:	It's Not Your Fault!
Lesson Timeframe:	25-50 minutes (dependent upon grade level)

Summary
This lesson will help students understand that it is NEVER their fault *if or when* someone hurts them (physically, verbally, or emotionally) or violates their trust.

Guiding Question(s)
Who is responsible for the things "we" do? Can we make people do bad or hurtful things to us? Is it okay to feel afraid, betrayed, or embarrassed if someone hurts us or violates our trust?

Standards Assessed in the Learning Expedition		
Discipline	Standards	Long-Term Learning Targets
Health Education	HE.45.C.1.4 – Describe & identify ways to prevent childhood injuries and/or health problems (physically and emotionally).	Understand and practice the skill of being openly expressive about a problem or disagreeing with harmful or wrong behaviors/practices.

C.A.P.E. Curriculum Anchor Text(s): *Anchor texts are key texts read to support content and health education skills. A teacher's set of the anchor texts are highly recommended.*		
Title	Author/Illustrator	Text Type
"You Did It Not Me! Brave Brittany Speaks Up!"	Kandra Albury/Jamie Cosley	Instructional Fiction

C.A.P.E. Curriculum – Lesson(s) 13-16:
The Courageous Power of Using Your Voice

Title:	**Drug Use Awareness & Prevention – LESSON 14**
Grade level:	Pre-K – 5
Subject(s):	Health Education
Specific topic:	What to Do When a Family Member or Friend Violates Your Trust.
Lesson Timeframe:	25-50 minutes (dependent upon grade level)

Summary
This lesson will help students understand what they should do *when or if* someone they trust violates them.

Guiding Question(s)
What does it mean to be violated? What should you do if someone you trust violates you? Can you prevent the possibility of being violated?

Standards Assessed in the Learning Expedition		
Discipline	**Standards**	**Long-Term Learning Targets**
Health Education	**HE.45.C.1.4** – Describe & identify ways to prevent childhood injuries and/or health problems (physically and emotionally).	Understand and practice the skill of being openly expressive about a problem or disagreeing with harmful or wrong behaviors/practices.

C.A.P.E. Curriculum Anchor Text(s): *Anchor texts are key texts read to support content and health education skills. A teacher's set of the anchor texts are highly recommended.*

Title	Author/Illustrator	Text Type
"You Did It Not Me! Brave Brittany Speaks Up!"	Kandra Albury/Jamie Cosley	Instructional Fiction

C.A.P.E. Curriculum – Lesson(s) 13-16:
The Courageous Power of Using Your Voice

Title:	**Drug Use Awareness & Prevention – LESSON 15**
Grade level:	Pre-K – 5
Subject(s):	Health Education
Specific topic:	It's Not Tattling *When* You're Trying to Protect Yourself or Someone Else.
Lesson Timeframe:	25-50 minutes (dependent upon grade level)

Summary
This lesson will help students understand that it is okay to tell someone when they have been violated or escaped an attempted violation.

Guiding Question(s)
How does your voice protect you? What happens *when and if* someone hurts/violates you and you don't tell? Whose safety is most important yours or the *person who hurt or violated you?*

Standards Assessed in the Learning Expedition

Discipline	Standards	Long-Term Learning Targets
Health Education	**HE.45.C.1.4** – Describe & identify ways to prevent childhood injuries and/or health problems (physically and emotionally).	Understand and practice the skill of being openly expressive about a problem or disagreeing with harmful or wrong behaviors/practices.

C.A.P.E. Curriculum Anchor Text(s): *Anchor texts are key texts read to support content and health education skills. A teacher's set of the anchor texts are highly recommended.*

Title	Author/Illustrator	Text Type
"You Did It Not Me! Brave Brittany Speaks Up!"	Kandra Albury/Jamie Cosley	Instructional Fiction

C.A.P.E. Curriculum – Lesson(s) 13-16:
The Courageous Power of Using Your Voice

Title:	**Drug Use Awareness & Prevention – LESSON 16**
Grade level:	Pre-K – 5
Subject(s):	Health Education
Specific topic:	Be Courageous It's Your Super-Power!
Lesson Timeframe:	25-50 minutes (dependent upon grade level)

Summary
This lesson will help students recognize and embrace the power of being courageous in difficult or hurtful situations by speaking up and out about violations against them.

Guiding Question(s)
Why is your voice SO powerful against a violator's wrongdoing? Whose voice is more powerful YOURS or a violator's? What requires a great amount of COURAGE, speaking up or remaining silent?

Standards Assessed in the Learning Expedition		
Discipline	Standards	Long-Term Learning Targets
Health Education	**HE.45.C.1.4** – Describe & identify ways to prevent childhood injuries and/or health problems (physically and emotionally).	Understand and practice the skill of being openly expressive about a problem or disagreeing with harmful or wrong behaviors/practices.

C.A.P.E. Curriculum Anchor Text(s): *Anchor texts are key texts read to support content and health education skills. A teacher's set of the anchor texts are highly recommended.*		
Title	Author/Illustrator	Text Type
"You Did It Not Me! Brave Brittany Speaks Up!"	Kandra Albury/Jamie Cosley	Instructional Fiction

Courageous Conversations™

For Secondary Education

Topics:

* Avoiding or Overcoming Sexual Abuse

* Avoiding or Overcoming Bullies or Bullying Situations

* Avoiding Drug Use & Being Influenced by Others with the Pressure of Trying Drugs.

C.A.P.E. Curriculum COURAGEous Conversations™ for Secondary Education

COURAGEous conversations™ are designed for students between the ages of 12-18. These discussions are collaborative and socially engaging to help maintain the student's interest in each lesson. The guided conversations are meant to specifically help students examine their actions and behaviors as well the actions and behaviors of others [family, friends, or simply individuals encountered in social settings]. Detailed below are COURAGEous Conversation Lesson Specifications & Activities.

COURAGEous Conversation™: How to Avoid or Overcome Sexual Abuse

Standards:

HE.6.C.1.2 – Describe how the physical, mental/emotional, social, and intellectual dimensions of health are interrelated.

HE.7.C.1.1 – Compare and contrast the effects of healthy and unhealthy behaviors on personal health, including sexual and emotional health.

HE.7.C.1.4 – Describe ways to reduce or prevent injuries and adolescent health problems.

HE.678.C.1.4 – Identify, describe, and investigate ways to reduce or prevent harm/injuries and adolescent health problems- emotionally, socially, and physically.

HE.8.C.1.2 – Analyze the interrelationship between healthy/unhealthy behaviors and the dimensions of health: physical, mental/emotional, social.

HE.912.C.1.1 – Predict how healthy behaviors can affect health status.

HE.912.C.1.4 – Propose strategies to reduce or prevent injuries and health problems.

HE.912.C.1.8 – Assess the degree of susceptibility to injury, illness or death if engaging in unhealthy/risky behaviors.

COURAGEous Conversation™ Guiding Essential Questions/Statements:

1. Define sexual abuse?
2. Who is susceptible [at risk] to the reality of sexual abuse or sexual crimes?
3. How can You avoid situations that are harmful sexually [emotionally & physically]?
4. Be Courageous! Courage is Your Super-Power!

Lesson Plan:

Direct Teaching/Introduction to the Lesson: Start each conversation by prompting student engagement and thinking with the guiding questions. Allow the students to answer. Introduce the specified topic, identify the DYDTMT [Don't You Dare Touch Me There] Zones, and pass around the "Capes of Courage." Stop and check for student understanding, pause if any students seem confused and ensure their comprehension throughout the COURAGEous Conversation.

Collaborative Learning and/or Independent Learning:

Activity 1: Independent Learning: Climate Survey {anonymous} "Did You Know This About Sexual Abuse?"

Activity 2: Interactive Group Discussion: "Speak Up"- Having COURAGEous Conversations: discuss scenario(s) listed below. Then have students hypothetically act out or tell what they would do in each situation. Also encourage students to come up with their own scenarios.

- ☐ Break into groups
- ☐ Give your group a fun name!
- ☐ One spokesperson for the group (adult or student)
- ☐ Spokesperson will offer courageous solutions
- ☐ You have 20 minutes! Let's get started

COURAGEous Conversation ™ #1

I'm Briana and I am 12-years-old. My Uncle Roy (short for Leroy) is my mom's older brother. He's 50-something-years-old and everybody seems to love him. But he tickles me and my little cousins in inappropriate places. In fact, he did it to some other kids and their friends during my mom's 42nd birthday barbeque last Saturday. It was held at my Aunt Pangie's house. He does this every time he comes around and I hate it! In fact, I try to hide from him whenever I see him. You can look at everyone's face and tell they don't like it either when he tickles them. I'm over it!

Stop. Think. Respond.

- ☐ How is Briana feeling/How do you think the other girls feel? How would you feel?
- ☐ What should the adults say to Uncle Roy?
- ☐ What should the kids say/do?
- ☐ What should Briana's mom have already said, to her, about this kind of situation?

COURAGEous Conversation ™ #2

Darrin is 15-years-old and participates in advanced performing arts at The Mets School of Performing Arts. Darrin has been playing piano since he was eight-years-old. One day Darrin stayed late working on chords for the annual spring production; he was going to audition for a solo part. After practice, Darrin received a text from him mom saying she was running late and it was starting to get dark. Mr. Brady decided to give Darrin a ride home, since he lived right around the corner from the school. During the drive, Mr. Brady told Darrin that he's intelligent and handsome. He also asked Darrin if he had a girlfriend. Darrin said no. Then he pulled over onto the side of the road and said if he doesn't have a girlfriend then he must have a boyfriend. This made Darrin uncomfortable. Darrin asked Mr. Brady if he could just keep driving. However, before continuing the drive, Dr. Brady showed Darrin inappropriate pictures in his cell phone. He recognized a kid in one of the photos. Darrin's heart started racing. Mr. Brady said, "to keep their conversation between the two of them, especially if he wants the solo part for the spring recital."

Stop. Think. Respond.

- How is Darrin feeling?
- What do you think Mr. Brady showed Darrin on the phone?
- Should Darrin tell his mom what happened?
- If it were you, would you tell your mom? Why/why not?
- What conversation should his mom or any responsible adult should have had with Darrin about this type of situation?

COURAGEous Conversation ™ #3

Cameron, nine-years-old, is taken to Ms. Simone, her baby sitter, when her mom and dad goes on their monthly date night. Now Ms. Simone, age 16, is not to have company over when her mom isn't home but whenever Cameron is dropped off, she calls her boyfriend over. He comes to the house and they go in her room and close the door. Cameron feels afraid when left in the living room to watch TV alone. Cameron doesn't like going over there anymore and besides, her boyfriend, Darrius calls her "lil' momma" and licks his lips and winks at her when sees her.

Stop. Think. Respond.

- How does Cameron feel?
- What should Cameron do?
- What type of conversations should Cameron's parents have already had with her about this kind of situation?
- How do you feel this situation should be handled?

COURAGEous Conversation ™ #4

Macy, 15, has been acting out in school, talking back, getting into fights and her grades have fallen. She told you (her BFF) what was happening. Her mom's boyfriend has been touching on her inappropriately when her mom's at work on the night shift at the local hospital. She said it has been going on for about two months now. It's been a week and you want to tell but Macy made you pinky promise not to. What do you do?

Stop. Think. Respond.

- How is Macy feeling?
- What would you do?
- What should Macy's mom have already said about this kind of situation?

COURAGEous Conversation ™ #5

Sherell is 10 and her older sister Sacoya is 14. Sherell asked her to keep a secret and told Sacoya that their mom's new live-in boyfriend, Ronald, looks at her strange. Sherell said he licks his lips and looks at her the same exact way, too. In fact, Sacoya told Sherell that the other day he rubbed up against her in the hallway when there was more than enough room for him to get past her. Their mom works swing shift at the local hospital and they don't feel safe when their mom isn't home.

The girls are devising a plan to runaway together to their Aunt Pangie's house. She lives almost five miles from where they stay. One day they agreed to just walk to their aunt's house while their mom was at work and Ronald was playing video games in the living room...

Stop. Think. Respond.

- How are the girls feeling?
- What boundaries should the mom have already put in place?
- When they tell their aunt how they feel about Ronald, how should she respond?
- If you were Aunt Pangie, what will you tell the girls? If you were the older sister, what would you say to your younger sister?

COURAGEous Conversation ™ #6

He noticed 14-year-old-Miles is the last child waiting for a ride following Easter rehearsal. He offers him a ride since he only lives a few streets over from his house. Miles also noticed little boys over at Deac.'s house and he thinks something isn't right. Miles called his mom and she said she was running late and to get the ride home with Deac. Duncan. Upon getting into the car, Deac. asked Miles if he had a girlfriend. Miles said no…Then Deac. shows him pictures of naked boys in his cell phone and asked what he thought of that. He noticed one of the boys from his second period lunch…

Stop. Think. Respond.

- What is Miles thinking?
- What is he possibly struggling with?
- What should Miles do/say?
- Is there a legal issue surrounding this matter?
- What things should his mom have already talked to him about?

COURAGEous Conversation ™ #7

Michael and Krystal have been secretly dating for about six months. During the summer, Michael stays with his dad up north. He texted Krystal and said he missed her. He asked her to send him some pictures, so she did. He texted her back and said "Not those, pics. Some in your birthday suit." Krystal was reluctant to send nude photos of herself, but she really likes Michael....

Stop. Think. Respond.

- How is Krystal feeling?
- Should she send the pictures? Why/why not?
- If she sends the pictures is this legal? If so, what is this called?
- Should Krystal continue in the relationship with Michael?
- What conversations should her parents have already had with her about this type of situation?

Activity 3: Independent Practice/Collaborative Discussion: "Courageous Declarations" have students complete the corresponding activity sheet. Students will write and recite various ways to say "I've been violated!"

Activity 4: Cooperative Learning: Students will complete "The Promise to Listen & Tell Agreement."

Cooperative Closure for the Lessons: Have the students journal or openly discuss their feelings regarding the lessons. If the students desire to share, encourage them to do so. Observe student reactions to the lessons, and remember your classroom should be a safety zone for all students.

C.A.P.E. Curriculum COURAGEous Conversations™ for Secondary Education

COURAGEous Conversations ™ are designed for students between the ages of 12 -18. These discussions are collaborative and socially engaging to help maintain the student's interest in each lesson. The guided conversations are meant to specifically help students examine their actions and behaviors as well the actions and behaviors of others [family, friends, or simply individuals encountered in social settings]. Detailed below are COURAGEous Conversation ™ Lesson Specifications & Activities.

COURAGEous Conversation™: How to Avoid or Overcome Bullies or Bullying Situations

Standards:

HE.6.C.1.2 –   Describe how the physical, mental/emotional, social, and intellectual dimensions of health are interrelated.

HE.7.C.1.1 –   Compare and contrast the effects of healthy and unhealthy behaviors on personal health, including sexual and emotional health.

HE.7.C.1.4 –   Describe ways to reduce or prevent injuries and adolescent health problems.

HE.678.C.1.4 – Identify, describe, and investigate ways to reduce or prevent harm/injuries and adolescent health problems- emotionally, socially, and physically.

HE.8.C.1.2 –   Analyze the interrelationship between healthy/unhealthy behaviors and the dimensions of health: physical, mental/emotional, social.

HE.912.C.1.1 – Predict how healthy behaviors can affect health status.

HE.912.C.1.4 – Propose strategies to reduce or prevent injuries and health problems.

HE.912.C.1.8 – Assess the degree of susceptibility to injury, illness or death if engaging in unhealthy/risky behaviors.

COURAGEous Conversation™ Guiding Essential Questions/Statements:

1. Define the term bullying?

2. Who is susceptible [at risk] to the reality of being a bully or being bullied?

3. How can You avoid situations that are viewed as bullying [verbally, emotionally, physically]?

4. Be Courageous! Courage is Your Super-Power!

Lesson Plan:

Direct Teaching/Introduction to the Lesson: Start each conversation by prompting student engagement and thinking with the guiding questions. Allow the students to answer. Introduce the specified topic, identify the various types or examples of bullying, and pass around the "Capes of Courage." Stop and check for student understanding, pause if any students seem confused and ensure their comprehension throughout the COURAGEous Conversation.

Collaborative Learning and/or Independent Learning:

Activity 1: Independent Learning: Climate Survey {anonymous] – "Did You Know This About Bullying?"

Activity 2: Interactive Group Discussion: "Speak Up"- Having COURAGEous Conversations™: discuss scenario(s) listed below. Then have students hypothetically act out or tell what they would do in each situation. Also encourage students to come up with their own scenarios.

- ☐ Break into groups
- ☐ Give your group a fun name!
- ☐ One spokesperson for the group (adult or student)
- ☐ Spokesperson will offer courageous solutions
- ☐ You have 20 minutes! Let's get started

COURAGEous Conversation ™ #1

Tiana is in 9th grade at Blues Creek High School and she's been being bullied since seventh- grade by Malasia. However, Malasia always hangs with a click of other girls who maliciously antagonize Tiana. They tell others not to sit with her at lunch, make fun of her hair and clothes. However, one of the girls in the click, named Nikki, isn't as mean as the other girls. Nikki is also on the dance team with Tiana at her church. Deep inside Tiana feels there's no use, especially since the bullying has been going on for two years now...

Stop. Think. Respond.

- ☐ How is Tiana feeling/How do you think the other girls feel? How would you feel?
- ☐ What should the adults say to Malasia?
- ☐ How do you think Nikki is feeling?
- ☐ What should Tiana's mom have already said about this kind of situation?

COURAGEous Conversation ™ #2

Cameron is a 10th grader at Eastside High School, and his friend Amos is a ninth-grader. Amos is always being teased and called a girl by Devin and his crew. Cameron encourages Amos to ignore those punks. However, Amos said he's sick and tired of the bullying and wants to kill all of them. He told Cameron his dad keeps a gun in the top of the closet. In fact, last summer, his dad showed him how to use it. Amos said he'll use it just to scare them...

Stop. Think. Respond.

- ☐ How does Cameron feel?
- ☐ What should Cameron do?
- ☐ How does Amos feel?
- ☐ What type of conversations should Amos's parents have already had with him about this kind of situation?
- ☐ How do you feel this situation should be handled?
- ☐ What could be the outcome if Amos follows through?

COURAGEous Conversation ™ #3

Rebecca, is a senior at BHS and love Snap Chat and Instagram. One day she noticed a group of girls and boys were bullying her friend Myisha's little sister who has Downs Syndrome. They were calling her "retard" and other unkind names in the comments. When Rebecca arrived at school the next day, people were calling her names. She asked them to stop but they wouldn't…

Stop. Think. Respond.

- ☐ How is Rebecca feeling?
- ☐ What would you do?
- ☐ What should Rebecca's mom have already said about this kind of situation?
- ☐ How is Myisha feeling (Rebecca's friend about the situation)?

COURAGEous Conversation ™ #4

Brandon, a Westwood Middle School 8th grader, sometimes has to ride the bus home with high school students. The high schoolers pick on him at times even at the bus stop when he gets off the bus. He told his mom over dinner that he's over it and stormed off to his room. He yelled, he 'wish he was dead'…

Stop. Think. Respond.

- ☐ How is Brandon feeling?
- ☐ What should the bus driver do, if anything at all?
- ☐ What should his mom do, if anything at all?
- ☐ True or False…Bullying at the bus stop isn't the school's responsibility.

Activity 3: Independent Practice/Collaborative Discussion: "Courageous Declarations" have students complete the corresponding activity sheet. Students will write and recite various ways to say "I won't be a bully, or allow other's to be bullied!"

Activity 4: Cooperative Learning: Students will complete "The Promise to Listen & Tell Agreement."

Cooperative Closure for the Lessons: Have the students journal or openly discuss their feelings regarding the lessons. If the students desire to share, encourage them to do so. Observe student reactions to the lessons, and remember your classroom should be a safety zone for all students.

C.A.P.E. Curriculum COURAGEous Conversations™ for Secondary Education

COURAGEous Conversations ™ are designed for students between the ages of 12 -18. These discussions are collaborative and socially engaging to help maintain the student's interest in each lesson. The guided conversations are meant to specifically help students examine their actions and behaviors as well the actions and behaviors of others [family, friends, or simply individuals encountered in social settings]. Detailed below are COURAGEous Conversation ™ Lesson Specifications & Activities.

COURAGEous Conversation™ : How to Avoid Drug Use & Being Influenced by Others with the Pressure of Trying Drugs.

Standards:

HE.6.C.1.2 –   Describe how the physical, mental/emotional, social, and intellectual dimensions of health are interrelated.

HE.7.C.1.1 –   Compare and contrast the effects of healthy and unhealthy behaviors on personal health, including sexual and emotional health.

HE.7.C.1.4 –   Describe ways to reduce or prevent injuries and adolescent health problems.

HE.678.C.1.4 – Identify, describe, and investigate ways to reduce or prevent harm/injuries and adolescent health problems- emotionally, socially, and physically.

HE.8.C.1.2 –   Analyze the interrelationship between healthy/unhealthy behaviors and the dimensions of health: physical, mental/emotional, social.

HE.912.C.1.1 – Predict how healthy behaviors can affect health status.

HE.912.C.1.4 – Propose strategies to reduce or prevent injuries and health problems.

HE.912.C.1.8 – Assess the degree of susceptibility to injury, illness or death if engaging in unhealthy/risky behaviors.

COURAGEous Conversation™ Guiding Essential Questions/Statements:

1. Why is drug-use detrimental to your overall health?
2. Who is susceptible [at risk] to the reality of being influenced to participate in drug use?
3. How can you avoid situations or people that include drug use?
4. Be Courageous! Courage is your Super-Power!

Lesson Plan:

Direct Teaching/Introduction to the Lesson: Start each conversation by prompting student engagement and thinking with the guiding questions. Allow the students to answer. Introduce the specified topic, identify drug categories [Illegal & Over the Counter], and pass around the "Capes of Courage." Stop and check for student understanding, pause if any students seem confused and ensure their comprehension throughout the COURAGEous Conversation ™.

Collaborative Learning and/or Independent Learning:

Activity 1: Independent Learning: Climate Survey {anonymous] – "Did You Know This About Adolescent Drug Use?"

Activity 2: Interactive Group Discussion: "Speak Up"- Having COURAGEous Conversations™: discuss the scenario(s) listed below. Then have students hypothetically act out and tell what they would do in each situation.

- ☐ Break into groups
- ☐ Give your group a fun name!
- ☐ One spokesperson for the group (adult or student)
- ☐ Spokesperson will offer additional courageous solutions
- ☐ You have 20 minutes! Let's get started

COURAGEous Conversation ™ #1

Bre'Shayla and Taylor are going to a party after the football game Friday night. It's going to be on and poppin' and everyone is going to be there from GHS and BHS. Bre'Shayla heard that there will be some vaping going on and that's all. Taylor said her sister let her try an edible (marijuana that you eat) the other day and it wasn't bad. She said there's nothing wrong with it and Bre'Shayla should try it because everyone has either smoked weed or eaten it before…

Stop. Think. Respond.

- ☐ How is Bre'Shayla feeling?
- ☐ What would you do?
- ☐ What should Bre'Shayla's parents have already said about this kind of situation?
- ☐ What advice should Bre'Shayla offer Taylor *if* any at all?
- ☐ Should Bre'Shayla just not go to the party?

COURAGEous Conversation ™ #2

Michael was hanging out with is friend Charlie and EJ following band practice at Eli Miller High School. Michael plays the trumpet, EJ plays the sax and Charlie plays the base drum. On their walk home, EJ pulled out a vaping device and started using it. Michael warned EJ that he shouldn't be vaping because it's bad for his lungs, especially when it comes to playing the sax. Charlie said, everyone has a habit and his is taking his dad's prescription pain pills…they help him to relax. EJ said he doesn't need Michael preaching to him like his parents. And besides, vaping is safer than smoking cigarettes. Michael, feels outnumbered and says, yeah and keeps walking with his friends.

Stop. Think. Respond.

- ☐ How is Michael feeling?
- ☐ Is vaping safer than smoking cigarettes
- ☐ What advice would you give Michael for his friends?

- Are taking someone else's medication safe? Why/ why not?
- https://www.youtube.com/watch?v=hI473QvlK24
- https://www.cbsnews.com/news/teens-hospitalized-for-lung-damage-after-vaping-e-cigarettes-juul-health-risks/

COURAGEous Conversation ™ #3

Tory and Sydney have been friends since kindergarten. They are now in seventh grade at Parkersview Middle. One day, while hanging out at their friend Tristan's house, Tristan took out Smarties (candy), crushed them and began snorting them like it was cocaine. Tory told him that it couldn't be good for him. Tristan said 'it's safer than snorting real cocaine and it's harmless'. Sydney said, 'it's just not cool…and what if your parents found out?!' Tristan told Sydney to 'shut up'. Sydney grabbed her backpack and told Tory 'let's get out of here!' Tory pauses…

Stop. Think. Respond.

- How is Sydney feeling?
- What could Tory be thinking?
- Is there anything wrong with snorting crushed smarties?
- What advice would you offer Tristan if any at all?
- https://www.youtube.com/watch?v=AWAT0zVP8Wc

Activity 3: Independent Practice/Collaborative Discussion: "Courageous Declarations" have students complete the corresponding activity sheet. Students will write and/or recite various ways to say "I won't use drugs or try to convince others to do them!"

Activity 4: Cooperative Learning: Students will complete "The Promise to Listen & Tell Agreement."

Cooperative Closure for the Lessons: Have the students journal or openly discuss their feelings regarding the lessons. If the students desire to share, encourage them to do so. Observe student reactions to the lessons, and remember your classroom should be a safety zone for all students.

APPENDICES

A	DYDTMT Zones Information Sheet	39
B.	DYDTMT Zones - Identification Activity Sheet (Girls)	40
C.	DYDTMT Zones - Identification Activity Sheet (Boys)	41
D.	Different Types of Bullying – Identification Activity Sheet	42
E.	How Drugs Affect Your Body – Identification Activity Sheet	43
F.	Snitching/Tattling Versus Telling – Identification Activity Sheet	44
G.	COURAGEous™ Declarations (Body Safety)	45
H.	COURAGEous Tween Talk ™ Q&A	46
I.	COURAGEous™ Declarations (Anti-Bullying)	47
J.	COURAGEous™ Declarations (Anti-Drug Abuse)	48
K.	Parental Permission Slip	49
L.	The Promise to Tell & Listen Agreement ("Don't You Dare Touch Me There!")	50
M.	The Promise to Tell & Listen Agreement ("Leave Us Alone You Mean 'Ole Bully!")	51
N.	The Pledge to be Drug Free ("NO… And I Mean No! Let's Say No to Drugs!")	52
O.	The Promise to Tell & Listen Agreement (Be COURAGEous™ – Speak Up and Speak Out!)	53
P.	My Heroic Rights to be Brave!	54
Q.	Songs & Chants to enCOURAGE	55
R.	Statistical Data Regarding Children About Sexual Abuse, Bullying, & Drug Usage	56
S.	Resources for Help	57

Student's Name: _____   Date: _____

Don't You Dare Touch Me There (DYDTMT) Zones Information Sheet

There are four (4) DYDTMT Zones, the descriptions below thoroughly explain where these zones are so that children will know these areas are off limits and that it is inappropriate for anyone to touch them!

ZONE 1: Mouth - Only food, drinks, or medicine(s) given to you by a responsible adult goes in here. What's your favorite or least favorite food?

ZONE 2: Chest [boys] & Breasts [girls]

ZONE 3: The Lower Frontal Area of Your Body/Private Parts – the Genital Area.

ZONE: 4: The Back of Your Body – Buttocks, Bottom, Butt, or Behind

DON'T YOU DARE TOUCH ME THERE ZONES! ™

FRONT   BACK

Student's Name: _____   **Date:** _____

DYDTMT Zones - Identification Activity Sheet (Girls)

Directions: Draw a circle to the four "Don't You Dare Touch Me There" Zones. Then color-code the pictures with the colors detailed below. Think about a traffic light when you think about good touch as [green], uneasy [yellow] bad/unwanted [red].

Red: This color is used to describe unwanted touch or breaking personal space/boundaries.

Yellow: This color is used to describe touching that makes you feel uncomfortable, uneasy or unsafe.

Green: This color is used to describe Good touch. Examples of good touch include a high five, fist bump, pat on the upper back or a pat on the head.

Always remember people should ask for permission to touch you, and it is OK to say NO even to trusted adults. It's your body and your voice...protect it!

FRONT

BACK

Student's Name: _____   Date: _____

DYDTMT Zones - Identification Activity Sheet (Boys)

Directions: Draw a circle to the four "Don't You Dare Touch Me There" Zones. Then color-code the pictures with the colors detailed below. Think about a traffic light when you think about good touch as [green], uneasy [yellow] bad/unwanted [red].

Red: This color is used to describe unwanted touch or breaking personal space/boundaries.

Yellow: This color is used to describe touching that makes you feel uncomfortable, uneasy or unsafe.

Green: This color is used to describe Good touch. Examples of good touch include a high five, fist bump, pat on the upper back or a pat on the head.

Always remember people should ask for permission to touch you, and it is OK to say NO even to trusted adults. It's your body and your voice...protect it!

41

Student's Name: _____   Date: _____

Different Types of Bullying – Identification Activity Sheet

Directions: Look at the illustrations/pictures below and identify the type of bullying that is illustrated in the picture.

Cyberbullying: The use of electronic communication to bully a person, typically by sending messages of an intimidating or threatening nature.

Physical Bullying: The use of one's body and physical bodily acts to exert power over peers. Punching, kicking, and other physical attacks are all types of physical bullying.

Verbal Bullying: When an individual uses verbal language (e.g., insults, teasing, etc.) to gain power over his or her peers.

Relational/Social Bullying: A form of bullying common amongst youth, but particularly so among girls, and involves a bully trying to hurt a peer and/or that peer's standing within a particular peer group.

Student's Name: _____   Date: _____

How Drugs Affect Your Body – Identification Activity Sheet

Directions: Looking at the pictures below, provide a caption that describes what the pictures might be depicting. Remember drugs ARE NOT good for your health at all!

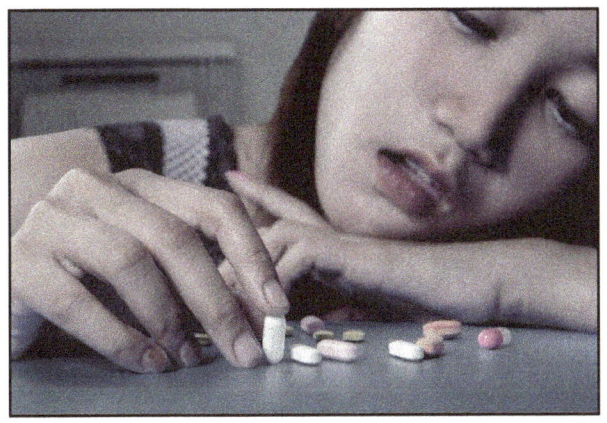

_____   _____

_____

STOP. THINK. RESPOND.

Is there help for these high school students? If so, what would you recommend? Let's discuss.

Student's Name: _____ **Date:** _____

Snitching/Tattling Versus Telling – Identification Activity Sheet

Directions: Looking at the picture below, provide a caption that says "Snitching/Tattling" or "Telling". Describe what you believe could be happening.

_____

_____

_____

STOP. THINK. RESPOND.

Is snitching just name calling, slang or just a way of creating fear? Let's discuss.

Student's Name: _____   Date: _____

COURAGEous™ Declarations (Body Safety)

Directions: On the space provided below, write down different ways to STOP someone from touching YOU inappropriately in any of the Don't You Dare Touch Me There Zones/private areas.

Example: "I'm telling, it is NOT right for you to touch or to try & touch me there!"

Write your COURAGEous Declarations below:

1. _____
   _____
   _____
   _____

2. _____
   _____
   _____
   _____

3. _____
   _____
   _____
   _____

4. _____
   _____
   _____
   _____

5. _____
   _____
   _____
   _____

COURAGEous Tween Talk ™ Q&A

Guest DJ / Moderator: Time for a COURAGEous Tween Talk. So what is Tween Talk? It's having real and relevant conversations. How many of you are ready to be real? Put your hands together and let's get started!

APPLAUSE!!!

Guest DJ / Moderator: Start out with some seriously FUN questions… You have to rush up here (don't fall to answer questions). Let's begin with some COURAGEous Conversations ™! Everyone ready? Let's get started right after this (spins records for 3-5 minutes).

1. True or False: You have to come up here to answer the question: It is OK to keep secrets when you or someone you know is being hurt. T or F… Explain why.

2. By a show of hands, how many of you know the official names of your private parts? I'm not talking about nicknames (adults those should be used anyways). OK… That's GREAT!

3. THINKING QUESTION: It is OK to take inappropriate photos and text them to your friends. Why or Why not. Is this illegal? What is it called?

4. THINKING QUESTION: What things shouldn't you do and or/ share online?

5. THINKING QUESTION: Define boundaries/ personal space.

6. True or False: Your body is to be respected. Explain.

7. THINKING QUESTION: What can you say to someone who makes you feel uneasy or uncomfortable?

8. Volunteer needed: Tell us something that a parent or guardian has shared with you about body safety:

9. True or False: You have a right to feel safe at all times. Explain.

10. THINKING QUESTION: If someone you know is being violated in any way, what would you do? What if you're asked not to tell?

11. THINKING QUESTION: Is there a difference between telling, tattling and snitching?

12. What is the best body safety advice you can offer someone else?

Let's give it up for some COURAGEous Tweens and Teens!!!

Student's Name: _____   Date: _____

COURAGEous™ Declarations (Anti-Bullying)

Directions: On the space provided below, write down different ways to STOP someone from bullying YOU or SOMEONE else.

Examples: "Get OUT of my face, and go away!" "STOP trying to bully me!" "I'm telling right now!"

Write your COURAGEous Declarations below:

1. _____

2. _____

3. _____

4. _____

5. _____

Student's Name: _____   Date: _____

COURAGEous™ Declarations (Anti-Drug Abuse)

Directions: On the space provided below, write down different ways to refuse drugs that are offered to you.

Example: "Drugs mess up your brain, I believe I'll refrain!"

Write your COURAGEous ™ Declarations below:

1. _____

2. _____

3. _____

4. _____

5. _____

Parental Permission Slip

Greetings Parents/Guardians:

In an effort to help keep students safe at _____ Elementary School, this week students will learn about body safety, bullying and illegal drug use prevention.

If you do not want your child to participate in these interactive lessons, please sign and date below and return the form to your child's teacher.

Sincerely,

Principal _____

-------------------------- Cut here and return to school----------------------

I_____ (Parent name) do not want my

student _____ to participate.

www.kidsncapesinc.org

facebook
Instagram

The Promise to Tell & Listen Agreement

Don't You Dare Touch Me There!

I (student's name) _____ promise to always tell an adult when someone is hurting me or makes me uncomfortable.

I/We (parent(s)/guardian's name _____ promise to always listen and take immediate action when my child tells me that someone is hurting him/her.

Student's signature _____

Parent/Guardian's signature _____

Today's Date: _____

www.kidsncapesinc.org

The Promise to Tell & Listen Agreement

Leave Us Alone You Mean 'Ole Bully!

I (student's name) _____ promise to always tell an adult when someone is tries to bully me verbally, physically, socially, or on social media (cyberbullying).

I/We (adult or guardian's name) _____ promise to always listen and take immediate action when my child or any child tells me that someone is bullying him/her.

Student's signature _____

Parent/Guardian's signature _____

Today's Date: _____

www.kidsncapesinc.org

The Pledge to be Drug Free

NO! …And I Mean NO! Let's Say NO to Drugs!

Today, I (student's name) _____ pledge to be drug free. I will activate my superpower-courage and not give-in to peer pressure. I will also encourage my family and friends to say NO to drugs. I will stand and say it loud – I'm cool, drug-free, and proud!

I (adult's name) _____ pledge not to use illegal drugs and I will also maintain a drug-free environment and lifestyle in which I will be a positive role model for children.

Student's signature _____

Parent/Guardian's signature _____

Today's Date: _____

www.kidsncapesinc.org

Promise to Tell & Listen Agreement

Be COURAGEous™ – Speak Up and Speak Out!

I (student's name) _____ promise to always tell an adult when someone is hurting me or makes me uncomfortable.

I/We (parent(s)/guardian's name _____ promise to always listen and take immediate action when my child tells me that someone is hurting him/her.

Student's signature _____

Parent/Guardian's signature _____

Today's Date: _____

www.kidsncapesinc.org

My Heroic Rights to be Brave!

1. It is my right to always feel safe.

2. It is my right to always stand up for myself.

3. It is my right to always tell a responsible adult, immediately, if or when someone makes a me feel unsafe or uncomfortable.

Call: 1-800-4-A-CHILD or 911 to tell when you don't feel safe!

Students recite these rights aloud. Teachers share/display the poster in your classroom.

www.kidsncapesinc.org

Songs & Chants to enCOURAGE

If you're drug free and you know it!

* Sung to the tune of: *"If You're Happy and You Know It"*

If you're drug free and you know it, say hooray! - Hooray!
If you're drug free and you know it, say hooray! - Hooray!
If you're drug free and you know it, and you really want to show it,
If you're drug free and you know it say hooray!

   Replace hooray with:

- uh-huh
- I'm cool

Don't You Dare Touch Me There!

* Sung to the tune of: *"The Wheels on the Bus go Round and Round"*

Don't You Dare Touch Me There, touch me there or touch me there!
Don't You Dare Touch Me There or I'm going to tell on you!

   Be sure to point to the Don't You Dare Touch Me There Zones to reinforce learning while singing.

The COURAGE Chant!

I need C-O-U-R-A-G-E!
You need C-O-U-R-A-G-E!
We need C-O-U-R-A-G-E!
We need COURAGE! YES, WE NEED COURAGE!

   * *Have a different student lead the courage chant and do a little courage dance!*

Spread COURAGE!

I have courage in my heart and courage on my mind!
When I'm soaring around town I have courage all the time!

   Four claps then repeat!

When I say ...

When I say BE, you say BRAVE! – Be! – BRAVE! – Be! – BRAVE!
When I say STAND, you say UP! – Stand! – UP! – Stand! – UP!
When I say SPEAK, you say OUT! – Speak! – OUT! – Speak! – OUT!
When I say SOAR, you say HIGH! – Soar! – HIGH! – Soar! – HIGH!

Statistical Data Regarding Children About Sexual Abuse, Bullying, & Drug Usage

1. Ninety percent of children know or have been acquainted with their abuser.

2. Sixty percent of children are abused by someone the family knows and trusts.

3. Forty percent of children are abused by a stronger more powerful child.

4. Thirty percent of children are abused by a family member.

5. One in four girls and one in six boys are sexually abused by their 18th birthday.

6. An abuser can abuse up to 400 children before one of those children will tell.

7. Twenty-eight percent of U.S. students in grades six-12 have experienced bullying.

8. Approximately 30 percent of young people admit to bullying others in surveys.

9. Seventy percent of young people say they have seen bullying in their schools.

10. Fifteen percent of high school students (grades nine–12) were bullied online in the past year.

11. However, 55 percent of LGBTQ students have experienced cyberbullying.

12. The most common types of bullying are verbal and social. Physical bullying happens less often. Cyberbullying happens the least frequently.

13. Marijuana is the most abused drug among adolescents nationwide.

14. Children and teens who use alcohol and drugs are more likely to have a substance use disorder as adults.

15. There is a clearly distinctive link between depression and substance abuse.

16. Teens don't recognize the risks of smoking marijuana regularly.

17. Twenty-three percent of adolescents have consumed alcohol by eighth-grade.

18. Teenage substance abuse also includes using legal medications without a prescription.

19. Nationwide, the drug overdose death rate has more than doubled during the past decade among people aged 12 to 25, according to the most recent Trust for America's Health report.

20. Teen drug, alcohol, and tobacco use are at their lowest rates since the 1990s. Moreover, the use of prescription drugs, heroin, ecstasy (MDMA), cocaine, crack, sedatives, and abuse of inhalants among adolescents all decreased.

Resources for Help

- **Darkness to Light Organization**:
  1-866 – FOR – LIGHT or Text LIGHT to 741741

- **National Abuse Hotline**: 1-800-422-4453 (Nationwide)

- **National Drug Helpline**: 1-888-633-3239

- **radKIDS**: 844-radKids 723-5437

- Sexual/Physical Abuse: 1-800-96-ABUSE (Florida)

- Suspected/Known Abuse: 1-800-4-A-CHILD

- **The Victims of Crime Resource Center Hotline**: 1-800-VICTIMS (842-8467)

- REMEMBER: In emergencies **911** should <u>always</u> be the first number to dial when in immediate danger!

Works Cited

Albury, Kandra. *Don't You Dare Touch Me There!* Bug Love Books, 2013.

Albury, Kandra, and Cosley, Jamie. *Leave Us Alone You Mean Ole Bully!* Kandra Albury, 2016.

Albury, Kandra, and Cosley, Jamie. *No! ... And I Mean No, Let's Say No to Drugs!* Kandra Albury, 2015.

Albury, Kandra and Cosley, Jamie. *You Did It Not Me! Brave Brittany Speaks Up!* Kandra Albury, 2019.

CPALMS https://www.cpalms.org/Public/

"Child Sexual Abuse Prevention Darkness to Light." *Darkness to Light*, www.d2l.org/.

"Children's Safety Network." *Bullying Prevention | Children's Safety Network*, 1 Aug. 2018, www.childrenssafetynetwork.org/injury-topics/bullying-prevention.

"Common Core State Standards Initiative" http://www.corestandards.org/

Office of Adolescent Health. "Substance Use and Adolescent Development." *HHS.gov*, US Department of Health and Human Services, 29 Mar. 2019, www.hhs.gov/ash/oah/adolescent-development/substance-use/index.html.

Kandra C. Albury

Kandra Albury is an Alachua County author, children's advocate, literary coach and Darkness to Light Sexual Abuse Prevention Training Facilitator. She is also a certified radKIDS instructor.

Kandra is the Presidents and CEO of Kids'n Capes, Inc., a non-profit that serves as a catalyst to community members, donors and organizations to help prevent and raise awareness of sexual abuse, bullying and illegal drug use in children early on.

She is the senior vice-president of business affairs and development with NCF Diagnostics & DNA Technologies in Alachua, FL., a minority-owned and accredited DNA laboratory.

Kandra has a bachelor's degree in communication from the University of North Florida and a master's degree in mass communication from the University of Florida. She earned a Ph.D. in ministerial education from Truth Bible University.

In 2012, she published her memoir *"From Food Stamps to Favor"*. Immediately after publishing her first book, she released the signature book in her children's book series titled, *"Don't You Dare Touch Me There!"* This book has been read to more than 5,000 children and adults in Florida, Georgia, Texas and Colorado. Her literary and children's advocacy work has been featured in numerous print publications as well as on local, national and international television networks such as WCJB TV-20, WUFT, WJXT-Channel 4, African Network Television-ANTV (host of the Kids'n Capes Show) and Trinity Broadcasting Network (TBN); the largest Christian network in the world.

Kandra is married to James C. Albury, manager of the Kika Silva Pla Planetarium at Santa Fe College. They are the proud parents of three courageous children and grandparents of one courageous grandson.

For more information about Kids'n Capes, Inc. visit: **www.kidsncapesinc.org**.

www.ingramcontent.com/pod-product-compliance
Lightning Source LLC
Chambersburg PA
CBHW061113070526
44583CB00027B/3282